THE RENAISSANCE

Richard Spilsbury

Heinemann Library
Chicago, Illinois

Customer service 888-454-2279
Visit our website at www.heinemannraintree.com

Produced for Heinemann Library by
White-Thomson Publishing Ltd
Bridgewater Business Centre
210 High Street, Lewes
East Sussex BN7 2NH, U.K.

Edited by Clare Collinson and Megan Cotugno
Designed by Mayer Media Ltd
Original illustrations by Peter Bull Art Studio
Picture research by Amy Sparks and Clare Collinson
Originated by Chroma Graphics
Printed and bound in China by Leo Paper Products

13 12 11 10 09
10 9 8 7 6 5 4 3 2

Library of Congress Cataloging-in-Publication Data
Spilsbury, Richard, 1963-
   Renaissance art / Richard Spilsbury.
      p. cm. -- (Art on the wall)
   Includes bibliographical references and index.
   ISBN 978-1-4329-1372-4 (hc)
   1. Art, Renaissance--Juvenile literature. I. Title.
   N6370.S65 2008
   709.02'4--dc22

                         2008020357

Acknowledgments
The Publishers would like to thank the following for permission to reproduce photographs:
Bridgeman Art Library **pp. 5** (Louvre, Paris, France/Giraudon), **6** (Galleria degli Uffizi, Florence, Italy), **9** (Scrovegni (Arena) Chapel, Padua/Alinari), **11** (Villa Farnesina, Rome), **14** (Museo de Firenze Com'era, Florence, Italy), **15** (Galleria degli Uffizi, Florence), **16** (San Zaccaria, Castello, Venice/Cameraphoto Arte Venezia), **17** (Palazzo Pitti, Florence), **18** (Vatican Museums and Galleries, Vatican City), **19** (Palazzo Ducale, Mantua/Alinari), **21** (Kunsthistorisches Museum, Vienna, Austria), **23** (Graphische Sammlung Albertina, Vienna), **25** (National Gallery, London, U.K.), **28** (National Gallery, London), **31** (National Gallery, London), **33** (Private Collection, Japan, Peter Willi), **34** (National Gallery, London), **35** (The Trustees of the Weston Park Foundation, U.K.); Corbis pp. **10** (Gianni Dagli Orti), **12** (Bettmann), **22** (Massimo Listri), **27** (Arte & Immagini srl.).

Cover photograph: Raphael (Raffaello Santi), *St. Catherine of Alexandria* (ca. 1507), reproduced with permission of the Trustees of the National Gallery/Bridgeman Art Library.

The Publishers would like to thank Susie Hodge for her invaluable help in the preparation of this book.

Every effort has been made to contact copyright holders of material reproduced in this book. Any omissions will be rectified in subsequent printings if notice is given to the Publishers.

Contents

Some words are printed in bold, **like this.** You can find out what they mean by looking in the glossary.

What is Renaissance Art?

A woman gazes at you from the canvas. Her skin, hair, and clothing appear so real, you feel as if you could almost touch them. She looks calm and seems to be smiling faintly. In the background is a distant landscape, with a river and jagged mountain peaks. This remarkable portrait is one of the most famous paintings in the world. It is a work by Leonardo da Vinci, an artist who painted during the Renaissance, over 500 years ago.

Renaissance art is the name given to the outstanding paintings and sculptures that were created in Europe from the early fifteenth century to the mid-sixteenth century. The main artistic centers at this time were northern and central Italy and northern Europe.

Ancient inspiration

The word *Renaissance* means "rebirth" in French. In the fifteenth century in Italy, there was a revival of interest in the ideas, literature, and art of **classical** Greece and Rome. Scholars and artists began to study the artistic and intellectual achievements of these ancient cultures in new ways. This inspired a fresh way of thinking about the world and a rebirth of interest in all aspects of the arts and learning.

A new kind of art

During the Renaissance, talented artists created a new kind of art, which broke away from traditions of previous centuries. They developed new techniques that gave paintings the **illusion** of depth. They chose new subjects for paintings, including scenes from classical mythology. They celebrated the beauty of nature and the human form, and depicted figures in a **naturalistic** way.

Renaissance artists are still admired today for their great skill in painting, drawing, and sculpture. Among the best-known artists of the period are Leonardo da Vinci, Michelangelo Buonarroti, Titian, Raphael, and Jan van Eyck.

Artistic invention

The Renaissance period was a time of great artistic invention. These are some of the new techniques discovered at that time:
- the use of **perspective** in paintings to create the illusion of depth in a **flat** image
- the use of **oil paints**, which took longer to dry than earlier paints, so artists could work on their paintings for longer
- drawing directly from nature.

Taking it further

Reading this book will help you look at "art on the wall" in a new way. It will also give you lots of ideas for developing your own painting style. On pages 46–47, there are suggestions for how you can take your studies further. These pages also include details of websites where you can view paintings by Renaissance artists, as well as museums and galleries to visit.

Leonardo da Vinci, *Mona Lisa* (ca. 1503–06). The *Mona Lisa* is probably the most celebrated portrait of all time. It is famous for its mastery of technique and for the mysterious smile of the young woman.

Art Before the Renaissance

During the centuries leading up to the Renaissance, all aspects of life in Europe were dominated by the **Catholic Church**. Toward the end of this period, people began to change the way they thought about the world and artists expressed the changing times.

Religion in medieval Europe

The period before the Renaissance, from about CE 450 to 1450, is known as the **medieval** period, or the Middle Ages. The Catholic Christian faith was the dominant religion in Europe at this time.

Many monasteries, churches, and cathedrals were built during the medieval period as places of worship and learning about the Christian faith.

Duccio di Buoninsegna, *Madonna and Child (Rucellai Madonna)* (1285). This is a typical example of a late medieval religious painting. Look at how flat the figures seem in comparison with the figure portrayed in the *Mona Lisa* on page 5.

Art in places of worship

Artists were paid to decorate places of worship with images of Jesus Christ, the Virgin Mary, and saints. They created sculptures on the walls, around doors, and on tombs in churches and cathedrals. They also created ceiling **mosaics**, **stained-glass windows**, and small paintings on wooden panels known as **altarpieces**.

The main purpose of the religious images artists created at this time was to help people learn about the Christian faith and encourage them to worship. The images were not intended to show the everyday world or realistic-looking human beings with human emotions. Instead, events, stories, and people were depicted as **symbols** of religious belief. For this reason, scenes and figures were painted in a very **stylized** way rather than in a realistic way. Medieval paintings were typically very flat, which means they looked **two-dimensional** and did not have any sense of depth.

Changing attitudes

The fourteenth century was a time of change in Europe. One important change that took place was in the way people thought about the Catholic Church and its leaders, the **Popes**. In medieval times, the Popes were in charge not only of the Catholic Church, but also other parts of life, such as how society in Italy was organized. The Popes became very powerful, and rich from donations given to the Church.

Toward the end of the medieval period, many people began to see the Popes as corrupt, and more interested in making money than in guiding people in the Catholic faith. Because of this, the Catholic Church lost some of its influence and control over people. Many people in Italy increasingly looked to the leadership of powerful nonreligious leaders, such as dukes and rich merchants.

These changing attitudes led some artists to experiment with different ways of painting religious subjects. Also, instead of just producing religious art for places of worship, they began to choose new subjects for their paintings and create more works for wealthy dukes and merchants.

Work for artists

Medieval artists got most of their work as **commissions** from the Catholic Church. They were paid by the Church to create paintings or sculptures inside churches and cathedrals. Sometimes rich landowners paid artists to create art, such as stained-glass windows, in churches. The landowners would do this to prove their belief in God or to show off their wealth and power. Sometimes artists also made domestic art, such as tapestries for rich people's homes.

Frescoes

During the medieval period, artists revived the technique of painting **frescoes**, an art form that was widely used in classical times. Frescoes are created by painting directly onto freshly plastered walls or ceilings while the plaster is still damp.

There are many examples of frescoes from classical times in Pompeii, an ancient town in southern Italy that was buried by a volcanic eruption in CE 79. Frescoes from early medieval times are rare, but the art form was revived in the late thirteenth century by Cimabue, an artist from the Italian city of Florence.

Cimabue's surviving frescoes, such as the *Madonna and Child* in the Church of St. Francis in Assisi, Italy, show his skill in painting using this technique. Many great artists created frescoes during the Renaissance period, including Andrea Mantegna (see page 19).

New realism

At the beginning of the fourteenth century, Giotto di Bondone, a pupil studying art under Cimabue, started to paint in a new style. His figures looked more natural, with more lifelike proportions, and he used shading to make the paintings appear less flat. Giotto is regarded by many as the inventor of modern painting.

In many medieval paintings, figures were depicted with faces that looked very similar. However, Giotto showed figures with distinctive, individual faces. His paintings were religious, like other medieval works, but unlike other artists of the time, he depicted Christ and other biblical figures with faces that showed human emotion. He also showed clothing in a more realistic way, with folds of cloth revealing the shape of people's bodies. Giotto created very careful **compositions**, in which figures and other objects were arranged to help the viewer understand the picture.

How artists created frescoes

Before an artist began painting a fresco, a smooth surface would be prepared by coating the wall with several layers of plaster. The artist would then make a sketch on the wall. While the plaster was still damp or fresh (*fresco* in Italian), the artist would paint colored **pigments** on the wall. The pigments would soak into the plaster and become fixed as the plaster dried. If the artist made a mistake, they would have to cut out the plaster from parts of the image and start again!

The angled background gives a sense of depth to the painting.

Giotto di Bondone, *Lamentation Over the Dead Christ* (ca. 1305). Notice how Giotto has composed his painting carefully, angling the background in the painting diagonally to focus attention on the subjects.

People look individual and different from each other.

Revival!

There is no exact date when Renaissance art was first created. But during the first half of the fifteenth century, there was a cultural revival in Italy. Educated people started to challenge medieval ideas, using inspiration from ancient Greece and Rome. Gradually, artists transformed the way they depicted the world.

A new cultural beginning

Changes in the way society in Italy was organized, such as the loss of power of the Popes and the rise in importance of wealthy merchants, made many

Myron, *Discobolus* (second century BCE). This sculpture of a discus thrower is a Roman copy of a Greek original. It displays the ancient Greek sculptor's mastery of **anatomy**.

The nude

In medieval times, it was unthinkable for artists to depict naked people or nudes, because nakedness was considered shameful in Christianity. In ancient Greece, however, artists were admired for creating sculptures and paintings showing idealized nude human forms, especially those of male heroes, champion athletes, and gods. During the Renaissance, artists studied the techniques of classical artists, and idealized nude figures became an important feature of Renaissance art. Donatello's bronze sculpture of the biblical character David, created in the early fifteenth century, was the first nude sculpture created in Europe since Roman times.

people in Italy think about the world in a new way. Classical art and buildings in Italy and other parts of the former Roman Empire reminded people of Italy's great past, and inspired artists to study classical techniques. Works by classical writers were rediscovered and copied by Italian scholars.

The revival of interest in these ideas led artists to study and depict the natural world in a new way. They learned from the techniques of classical sculptors how to create more realistic images of people. Rather than just painting religious scenes as in the past, they chose new themes for their paintings, including scenes from classical mythology.

Classical proportions

Sculptures of figures in classical times were **idealized**. This means they had body proportions that made them look beautiful. Ancient Greek artists, whose work ancient Roman artists often copied, had written rules for how they should show ideal male beauty. For example, they said that the ideal length from the top of the head to the navel is the same as the length from the navel to the knee. Sculptures based on these ratios were not very realistic. Sculptures of women were generally slightly modified versions of idealized men, even though in reality women have different body proportions from men.

Raphael (Raffaello Santi), detail from *The Triumph of Galatea* (ca. 1512). Raphael painted the famous *Galatea* fresco at a villa in Rome, which was owned by a very wealthy banker. The fresco, depicting the mythological character Galatea, shows Raphael's skill in painting his idea of idealized beauty.

The classical idea of depicting idealized beauty was revived by Renaissance artists. However, figures in Renaissance works looked more naturalistic, because artists studied anatomy and the body proportions of real people.

Getting closer to nature

During the Renaissance, people were inspired by classical ideas about learning. They came to believe that in order to understand the world around them, they should investigate and study it for themselves and not rely on other people's interpretations. Artists began to study the natural world and the human form closely, so they could draw, paint, and sculpt what they saw as realistically as possible.

Leonardo da Vinci, drawings of the anatomy of a shoulder (undated). Leonardo based his drawings on his dissection of dead bodies.

For example, to understand the outside shape of a human body better, Leonardo da Vinci cut open dead bodies to study the layout of muscles and bones inside. At that time, people did not think of science and art as separate subjects. They saw them both as ways to investigate nature. Leonardo studied a wide range of scientific subjects, including anatomy, mathematical shapes, and the way machines work.

Sketchbooks

During the Renaissance, for the first time in art history, artists started to use sketchbooks for their designs, sketches, and ideas. They mainly did this to prepare for paintings or sculptures. Leonardo filled hundreds of sketchbooks with his drawings. He drew ideas for inventions, such as tanks or "war machines," helicopters, submarines, and floating bridges. He drew many different faces, people's hands, the shapes of different plants, and rock formations.

Leonardo's sketchbooks show how he tried out different styles of drawing. He believed artists should experiment as much as possible. He did not think there was a right or wrong way to paint or do anything else.

Leonardo actually finished only a few paintings and sculptures. But many subsequent artists and art students since that time have used sketchbooks to draw details and ideas of forms they see or imagine. Artists today still consider sketchbooks vital for experimenting with art and in preparing their finished artworks.

Try it yourself

Head sketch

It is tricky to sketch a human head so that it looks realistic. However, there is a simple trick for getting the proportions right. Why not try this yourself? Draw a circle and then add a jaw extending half the depth of the circle below it. This is the basic head shape. Then imagine the head is divided into three equal sections horizontally. The eyes are at the center of the middle third. The nostrils are at the bottom of the middle third, and the ears are in the middle third. The mouth is at the center of the bottom third.

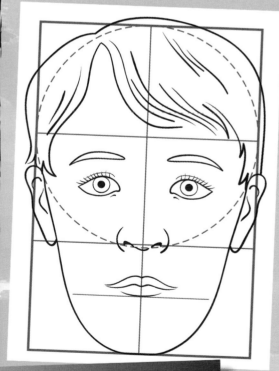

The proportions of a person's head vary from one person to another, but following the basic principles described above can help with the shape and position of the features in your drawings.

Giovanni Bellini, detail from an altarpiece in the Church of San Zaccharia, Murano, Venice (1505). Bellini's use of bright, warm colors makes the figure and the background appear to be bathed in light. Soft edges to different shapes in the image give it a hazy, tranquil feel.

Spreading through Italy

Florence was the most important center of Renaissance art throughout the fifteenth century, but by the beginning of the sixteenth century, other Italian cities, including Venice, Rome, and Mantua, had also become significant centers of the Renaissance art revolution.

Venetian artists

In Renaissance times, Venice was the most important city in Italy for trade with Asia. Silk, spices, and jewels from Asia were traded for wool, Venetian glass, and other European commodities. Venice is cut off from the mainland, since it is built on a series of islands stretching across a lagoon, separated by canals. It was ruled by the powerful **doge**.

The most famous Venetian painters were Giovanni Bellini and his pupils Titian and Giorgione. In their paintings, they used jewel-like colors, which seem to glow more brightly than the colors in Florentine paintings. The colors convey the special quality of the natural light in Venice, where sunlight shimmers off the canals and surrounding sea. Venetian artists sometimes added finely ground glass to their paint to help it reflect light. Giorgione is noted for painting dramatic, moody landscapes as backgrounds to his subjects. He captures the way changing weather, such as an approaching storm from the sea, affected light and colors in a scene.

Titian's contract

In 1516, Titian became the official artist of the doge of Venice. His annual wage of 60 ducats was worth about $1,200 in today's money. In addition to the wage, he received free board and lodging. For each likeness of the doge he painted, he was given an extra 4 ducats ($80). This does not sound like much, but many goods cost less in those days. For example, a bed cost about 1 ducat ($20).

Portrait master

Titian, whose real name was Tiziano Vecelli, worked in Venice and was a master of painting portraits. He painted a hundred images of popes, doges, and kings during his long life.

Titian often painted dark, plain, rich-colored backgrounds to focus attention on the subject. He carefully observed and painted the facial expressions of his subjects, so that we can imagine what their characters were like. Titian viewed his subjects neither from the front nor the side, as would have been common in medieval times, but instead, from a three-quarter view. He lit his subjects with strong light that brought out the shapes of their features and made their faces stand out more.

Titian (Tiziano Vecelli), *Portrait of a Noblewoman*, or *La Bella* (1536). Titian was an expert at painting the textures of fine fabrics and jewelry worn by his wealthy clients and models.

Michelangelo Buonarroti, *Creation of the Sun and Moon*, detail from the Sistine Chapel ceiling (1508–12). This detail from Michelangelo's world-famous fresco on the Sistine Chapel ceiling shows a Biblical scene in which God creates the Earth in six days. Michelangelo's God looks majestic, but his expression is that of a real person with real emotions, too.

New Roman art

For most of the fourteenth century, the Popes lived in France, but in 1377, they returned to Rome and the city became the center of the Catholic Church. Here, the Popes lived in a city-within-a-city called the Vatican. The most important building within the Vatican, after St. Peter's Cathedral, was the Sistine Chapel.

Pope Sixtus IV (1414–84) and Pope Julius II (1443–1513) commissioned the best artists in Italy, including Botticelli, Raphael, and Michelangelo Buonarroti, to decorate the inside of the chapel. Pope Julius commissioned Michelangelo to paint a fresco on the ceiling. This fresco, featuring beautifully painted figures and scenes from

The most famous ceiling in the world

Michelangelo was commissioned to paint the ceiling of the Sistine Chapel in 1508. He constructed special scaffolding to support him while he stood and painted, looking upward. It took four years for Michelangelo to paint the whole ceiling, which has an area of more than 4,000 square feet (400 square meters). The commission was originally to include 12 figures, but Michelangelo finally painted over 300! Michelangelo used bright, almost luminous colors, so the detail of the fresco could be seen from the floor 66 feet (20 meters) below. The painted figures are masterpieces of the Renaissance, with their muscular anatomy, their sense of movement, and the realistic expressions on their faces.

biblical stories, came to be one of the most famous artworks in the world. The German author, Goethe (1749–1832), said: *"Without having seen the Sistine Chapel, one can form no appreciable idea of what one man is capable of achieving."*

Family pictures

In Renaissance times, one of the most famous artists in Mantua, a city in northern Italy, was Andrea Mantegna. Some of Mantegna's best-known works are frescoes of his patrons, the Gonzaga family, who ruled Mantua. In Renaissance times, artists sometimes painted the families, friends, and contacts, or **court**, of their patrons. Such images were often commissioned to show the patrons' wealth and influence in society. Mantegna's speciality was painting his subjects from interesting viewpoints. He paints the Gonzaga family so that the viewer is slightly looking up to them, which emphasizes their power.

Andrea Mantegna, detail from *Ludovico Gonzaga, His Family, and Court* (ca. 1470). In this fresco, Mantegna shows the Gonzaga family group, some in mid-conversation, complete with a small woman who was a nanny to the children, and the family dog, Rubino.

Renaissance Art Outside Italy

During the Renaissance period, changes in the arts were also taking place in other parts of Europe, including the Netherlands, Belgium, and Germany. The term used to describe the Renaissance in these countries is the *Northern Renaissance*. Northern Renaissance paintings were often on a smaller scale than Italian frescoes and paintings, but they had great beauty in their detail and decoration.

Northern center of art

In Renaissance times, one of the wealthiest regions in Europe was Flanders, a region that extended from northern France to the northern part of the Netherlands, and it centered on such cities as Bruges in present-day Belgium. Like Florence, this region was a center of the wool trade. The French dukes who ruled the area, and merchants who had become rich through trade, commissioned local artists to create paintings for their homes and for churches.

An eye for detail

The Northern Renaissance painters did not have access to the Roman and Greek sculptures that the Italian Renaissance artists studied. This may explain why their figures are less like the classical ideal figures we see in Italian Renaissance art. Northern Renaissance figures are generally very realistic. Another characteristic of much Northern Renaissance art is very close attention to detail.

One of the best-known painters of the Northern Renaissance was Jan van Eyck, who spent most of his career in Bruges. He painted many small altarpieces for churches, as well as portraits of merchants and interior scenes from their city homes. His paintings are incredibly rich in detail.

Religious art in Northern Europe

Churches in Northern Europe had larger windows than churches in Italy. The windows were designed to let in enough weak northern light to illuminate the inside of the church. This meant there was less wall space for large-scale frescoes than in Italian churches. Also, the weather in Northern Europe is colder and damper than in Italy, so frescoes on the walls of churches would get moldy before drying properly. For these reasons, Northern Renaissance church paintings were generally small, and Bible scenes were often depicted on wooden panels.

Pieter Bruegel the Elder, *Peasant Dance* (1568). Breugel captures the busy celebrations of people living in the Flanders countryside using rich colors and detailed expressions.

Van Eyck was an expert at painting the jewels and different fabrics worn by wealthy people, from velvet to fur, as well as the reflections on metal and stone surfaces in their dimly lit rooms. The richness of color seen in Van Eyck's paintings was partly made possible because of his innovative use of oil glazes (see pages 30–31).

Pieter Bruegel the Elder

Pieter Bruegel the Elder was one of the leading **Flemish** artists of the Northern Renaissance. He chose to paint scenes of village life and poor people in the countryside instead of the rich people of the court and Church. He depicted peasants hunting, celebrating, feasting, and working together in the fields. His paintings are very busy and detailed, and although they look fun, they usually have a moral tone. For example, his painting *Peasant Dance* depicts the celebration of a religious festival, but it also shows people displaying inappropriate behaviour for the day, such as fighting and kissing in public.

Imagining hell

The Dutch painter Hieronymus Bosch painted very distinctive paintings in an unusual style. Some of Bosch's works show disturbing images of what he imagined a Christian hell to be like.

Bosch came from a town in the Netherlands called 's-Hertogenbosch. He was a member of a religious organization there known as the Brotherhood of Our Lady. Bosch received many commissions to paint wooden panels in the main church of the group. One of his most famous paintings is a **triptych**, or painting in three panels, called *The Garden of Earthly Delights*. The left-hand panel shows Bosch's idea of Adam and Eve in paradise, and the bigger central panel shows nude figures, birds, fruit, and other people on Earth. The right-hand panel shows Bosch's idea of hell, filled with devils, knives, fires, strange creatures, and people in torment. Bosch's scenes are so realistic that they have sometimes been described as appearing like snapshots from a nightmare.

German masters

The German artist Albrecht Dürer is often said to be the greatest artist of the Northern Renaissance. He studied and drew from nature like Leonardo da Vinci. He was fascinated by the details and differences between living things. He drew meadow flowers, animals such as the hare and rhinoceros, and some self-portraits. He also painted altarpieces and other paintings, but complained that they took too long. Dürer is best known for his printed **engravings** and **woodcuts**. Engravings are images cut into copper plates with a sharp tool. Woodcuts are images carved into wooden blocks. In both cases, the cut-away parts hold no ink and appear white on the final print.

Hieronymus Bosch, detail of the central panel of *The Temptation of St. Anthony* (ca. 1500). Bosch intended his depictions of hell to make church visitors believe they should lead a good, Christian life in this world, or they might suffer in the next.

Hans Holbein

Another important Northern Renaissance artist was the German painter, Hans Holbein. Holbein started his artistic career painting religious scenes and religious leaders. He later moved to England and became a specialist portrait painter under the patronage of the royal court. His superbly detailed paintings of leaders such as King Henry VIII give us a window into the lives of people of **Tudor** times.

Albrecht Dürer, *Hare* (1502). Dürer's study of a hare shows his great interest in nature. It is painted using watercolors. Dürer was one of the first artists to work with watercolors.

Circulating art

In 1439, Johannes Gutenberg invented the printing press to print multiple copies of the Bible. This created demand from publishers for artworks that could be printed in books. Some prints, such as those by the German artist Dürer, were of very high quality and became appreciated throughout Europe. Printers then started to make and sell "Old Master prints" that were not in books. Other Renaissance artists, such as Raphael and Titian, who wanted their art to be circulated more widely, also employed printers to make woodcuts or engraved versions of their work.

Renaissance Art Techniques

Several very important artistic techniques were developed during the Renaissance period. These included the use of oil paints and a technique for giving images a sense of depth. These developments transformed art from that point in history onward.

Linear perspective

In Renaissance times, Florentine artists created a system called **linear perspective**. Linear perspective is used to create the illusion of depth in a flat painting. Artists use the technique to make two-dimensional shapes in a flat painting appear solid, and to make scenes appear to extend into the distance. Filippo Brunelleschi was an architect who first developed linear perspective in the early fifteenth century. The artist, Leon Alberti, wrote a book in 1435, explaining the rules of perspective.

How perspective works

The artist imagines the surface of a drawing or painting to be a window to see the painted world through. They draw a line to show the boundary between the land and the sky, usually at the eye level of the viewer. This is the **horizon line**. Then they decide on a point on the line that represents the farthest point they can see. This is the **vanishing point**. The artist then draws a series of parallel lines, or **orthogonal lines**, which all **converge** or meet at the vanishing point, a little like the way railroad tracks appear to join up in the distance.

Artists use orthogonal lines to guide their drawing. The lines help them draw objects in the distance smaller than those in the foreground. They also help artists to make the edges of buildings and other features angle toward the vanishing point.

Perspective master

The Italian Renaissance artist, Piero della Francesca, was a master of perspective. Many of his paintings have unusual compositions, as if he wanted to show off his perspective skills more than his subjects! During his lifetime, Piero was better known as a mathematician. He learned about math during his early education as a merchant's son and by studying ancient Greek books on mathematics. He wrote books with detailed instructions of how to draw tricky **geometric** shapes, such as spheres, pyramids, and cylinders with realistic perspective.

Going further

Look at the corner of a box from close up. You can see two sides of the box. The lines at the top and bottom of one side appear to converge toward one vanishing point, and the lines at the top and bottom of the other side converge toward another vanishing point. Some Renaissance artists used two or more vanishing points when they wanted to show more than one side of an object.

Artists often distort shapes to suggest depth. For example, feet look shorter when viewed from the end than when viewed from the side. This is called **foreshortening**.

orthogonals

vanishing point

Carlo Crivelli, *The Annunciation with St. Emidius* (1486). Artists such as Crivelli sometimes gave their paintings depth by aligning objects in their paintings with orthogonals. The angled lines of the walls in this painting form the orthogonals, which converge at the vanishing point.

Try it yourself

Drawing a room perspective

Try creating a picture of a room using the rules of perspective.

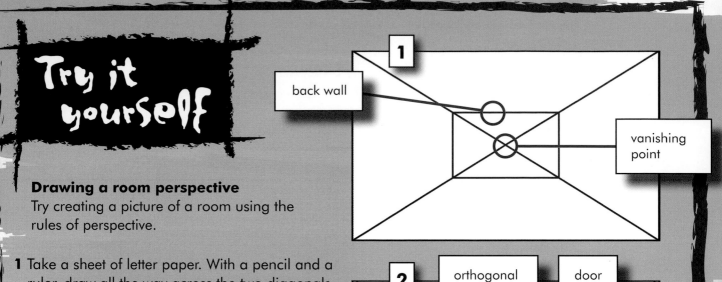

1 Take a sheet of letter paper. With a pencil and a ruler, draw all the way across the two diagonals of the page. The point where the two lines meet is the vanishing point. Draw a rectangle around the vanishing point. This rectangle forms the back wall of your room.

2 Now add a door on the right-hand side of the room. Starting near the bottom right of the page, draw a straight line up from the diagonal line, almost as far as the diagonal line at the top right. This forms one of the door's edges. Then draw an orthogonal guide line from the top of the door edge to the vanishing point. Use this orthogonal to help you add the other door edge.

3 Now add a window on the opposite side of the room. Draw a short vertical line midway between the two diagonal guide lines, but near the edge of the paper. Then draw orthogonal guide lines from the top and the bottom of this line. Use these lines to draw in the top and bottom of your window and join them to complete it.

4 Now add some other features, such as pieces of furniture and a rug, to the bottom section of the room. Use the same method of starting with an edge line and joining orthogonal guide lines to the vanishing point to help you.

5 Finish by erasing the orthogonal guide lines outside the features and the lines to the vanishing point within your back wall. You could also shade or color the features to make the room look even better.

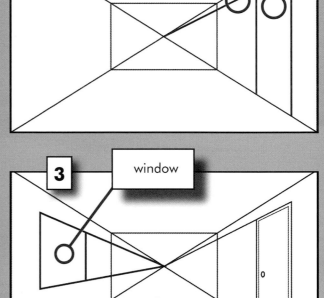

Sculpture and perspective

Renaissance sculptors also used perspective and foreshortening to make their figures seem more real. Great sculptors, such as Michelangelo and Donatello, always considered from which viewpoint their **three-dimensional** work would be seen, directly in front or from below, and at what distance.

Michelangelo altered the proportions of body features to make them appear more realistic when viewed from below. For example, he carved a stone sculpture of *David*, a boy who in the Bible story fought a giant, Goliath. David has unrealistically large hands and feet relative to the size of his head. His body is tense and muscular, and his serious expression shows us that David was determined to defeat his enemy.

Donatello invented a new way of sculpting called flattened **relief**. Using this technique, the design is partly "drawn" on the stone with a fine chisel and partly carved out. When this technique is used on pale stone—such as marble, in particular—it creates an illusion of depth, because of the way the carvings and lines reflect light and create shadows. Donatello's carved panels were designed to be mounted high up on the sides of pulpits in churches in Florence.

Michelangelo Buonarroti, detail of *David* (1504). Michelangelo believed that every stone had a sculpture within it, and that the work of sculpting was simply a matter of chipping off all that was not part of the statue.

Color perspective

Renaissance painters realized they could create an impression of depth or distance in a picture by using color and light. They carefully observed natural scenery and noticed that colors get lighter and also turn slightly bluer with increasing distance.

Artists also realized that when we view the natural landscape, the difference, or **contrast**, between color **tones** in the landscape appears to become less as the landscape becomes farther away. They also noticed that we see much less detail in objects that are far away, such as mountains or forests, than in objects that are near. Artists used these observations to paint images with a much greater sense of depth between the foreground and distance.

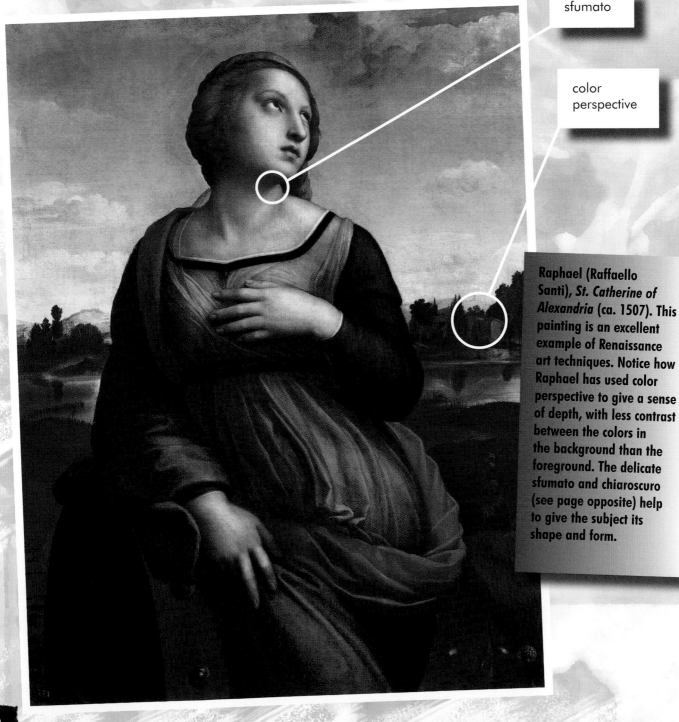

sfumato

color perspective

Raphael (Raffaello Santi), *St. Catherine of Alexandria* (ca. 1507). This painting is an excellent example of Renaissance art techniques. Notice how Raphael has used color perspective to give a sense of depth, with less contrast between the colors in the background than the foreground. The delicate sfumato and chiaroscuro (see page opposite) help to give the subject its shape and form.

Shading and chiaroscuro

Using linear and color perspective gives a sense of the position of objects in a painting. But to make an object appear solid and three-dimensional, artists also need to use shading. Shading helps to make an object look real by revealing how light falls across its surface. In the Renaissance, artists used different shades of colors in their paintings to show varying tones caused by light. By using contrasting light and dark tones, they made objects appear three-dimensional. This technique of emphasizing the form or shape of a figure or an object is called **chiaroscuro**.

Sfumato

Renaissance artists also used a technique called **sfumato**, an Italian word meaning "smoky." In this technique, thin glazes of oil are used to soften and blend the tones of color at the point where one tone changes to another. This gives an illusion of depth and softens the image to give an almost "smoky" effect. One of the best-known examples of the use of sfumato is in the *Mona Lisa* by Leonardo da Vinci (see page 5). Leonardo used the technique to make the corners of the woman's mouth soft and indistinct, blending them into shadow. This gives an atmosphere of mystery and the viewer is not quite sure of the woman's mood.

Try it yourself

The art of chiaroscuro
You can use shading to make a picture of a sphere. Put a ball on a table in a dimly lit room and light it from one side with a lamp. Draw the ball as a circle. Add shading to the half that is farthest away from the lamp. Now draw in the shadow that is cast by the ball. Then use an eraser to rub a thin band near the base of the ball, to show the light reflected from the table onto the ball. Imagine a spot on the ball closest to the lamp, which is brightly lit. This is the highlight. Then build up the shading gradually in circles around the highlight toward the shaded half of the ball, so the shading gets darker as it gets closer to the shaded half of the ball.

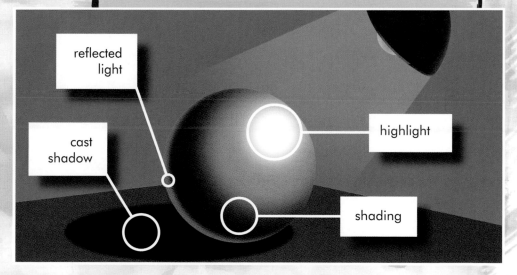

reflected light

cast shadow

highlight

shading

Egg tempera

In early Renaissance times, there was only one choice of paint artists could use on wooden panels. This was **egg tempera**, which was made by mixing color pigments with egg yolk. Painters or their assistants often made their own pigments by carefully grinding chunks of colored stone, dried earth, seashells, insects, and other materials into very fine powder. After the pigments were mixed with egg, the tempera dried quickly. This meant that artists had to work quickly on one small area of a painting at a time. The paint could also only be applied in thin layers.

New medium

In the fourteenth century, artists experimented with using colored oil as a varnish painted over egg tempera. Soon after this, however, the technique of oil painting was developed. The new **medium** became popular all over Renaissance Europe.

Try it yourself

Make your own paints

You can make paint by grinding up a large chalk stick. Seal the stick in a zipped plastic freezer bag and gently bash it with a hammer. Be careful to keep your fingers out of the way and work on a protected surface. Try to make the chalk powder as fine as possible so your paint isn't lumpy. Pour the powder into a bowl and add a teaspoon of water. Mix to a smooth paste with a Popsicle stick and then add 1 tablespoon of white craft glue. Finally, add water slowly until your paint doesn't drip, but will brush on smoothly. Then start painting!

The value of Renaissance art

In medieval times, the most highly prized art was usually the art that used the most expensive materials, such as expensive **gold leaf** or rare blue lapis lazuli pigment. Patrons would specify what materials could be used and how much time a painting should take. During the Renaissance, things gradually changed. Patrons offered more money for high-quality work, so the most skillful artists were the most highly paid. In medieval times, artists often painted groups of figures on plain backgrounds coated with gold leaf. They did this to make their work look expensive. In the Renaissance, artists were more interested in showing off their skills in perspective, foreshortening, and in depicting nature realistically.

Jan van Eyck, *The Arnolfini Marriage* (1434). Van Eyck perfected the use of oil paints to create subtle light effects, for example, on the gleaming brass chandelier. The Arnolfinis were an important family who lived in Flanders at that time.

Oil paint was made by mixing color pigments with linseed oil. One big advantage of oil paint is that it dries very slowly. This meant that painters could continue to blend colors, make changes, correct mistakes, and refine the details of their paintings days after they had first brushed the paint on. They could work on the whole picture at once, instead of doing it bit by bit.

Artists could also use oil paints to create different textures, for example, by layering thin glazes to build up intense colors or by adding thick daubs as color highlights on objects. By the sixteenth century, Renaissance artists were using oil paints on stretched canvases, especially in Venice, where artists could buy good-quality sail canvas to work on.

The Decline of Renaissance Art

During the sixteenth century, the Renaissance spread from Italy to the rest of Europe. However, from the mid-sixteenth century onward, great changes in the religious and political life of Europe were starting to eat away at the Renaissance influence, and eventually, artists began to take new directions.

Spreading ideas

One of the main ways in which Renaissance ideas spread from Italy and northern Europe to other parts of Europe was through books. Most cities in sixteenth-century Europe had printing presses, so printed books became cheaper and more widely available than hand-copied books. More people were learning to read, because more schools and colleges were being set up to educate people for careers in the Church and government. Their libraries stocked up on the latest books from Renaissance Italy and northern Europe, revealing the creativity and spirit of the age.

Not all countries influenced by Renaissance ideas produced as many great artists as Italy, but most produced equally important creativity. For example, the English Renaissance produced the world-famous writers, John Milton and William Shakespeare.

Changes in Europe

There were, however, other powerful influences spreading through Italy and Europe during the sixteenth century. Many people left the Catholic Church and became **Protestants** after reading the teachings of the Christian monk, Martin Luther. Protestants believe in the religious authority of the Bible and not that of Popes.

Bonfire of the vanities

Toward the end of the fifteenth century, a friar named Savonarola became powerful in Florence. He encouraged the people of Florence to be more religious, and preached against what he saw as the corruption of the clergy. He also preached against Renaissance ideas and told people to destroy objects such as books, mirrors, cosmetics, and paintings. He believed these were immoral distractions from religion that might encourage sin. He organized many public fires where people could burn their possessions. The bonfires were known as "bonfires of the vanities."

Luther criticized what he saw as the lavish decoration in churches, which was often paid for with money given to the Church by poor people. As Protestantism became more popular, artists did not receive so many commissions from the Church.

This period of tension between Catholics and Protestants coincided with a series of foreign invasions of Italy, and also wars between Italy and other countries. These wars brought the end of many city-states.

New art movement

Many artists responded to the changes and turmoil in society in the second half of the sixteenth century by taking new directions in art. Part of the need for change came because many of the greatest Renaissance artists, such as Raphael and Leonardo da Vinci, had died. Rather than try to match the excellence of these old masters, younger artists developed their own styles.

Mannerism is the name for the art movement in which artists developed recognizable, distinctive, and often unrealistic painting styles. For example, the Greek artist known as El Greco developed

El Greco, *The Annunciation* (ca. 1575). El Greco's painting is an example of Mannerism. This style of painting is noted for its unnatural light, unrealistic elongated figures, and unclear perspective. These characteristics set it apart from Renaissance art's realism and careful attention to perspective.

a very unrealistic style. He painted elongated people in unusual compositions using bright, garish colors and thick, obvious brushstrokes.

New realism

From the late sixteenth to the end of the seventeenth century, the Catholic Church's aim was to bring people back to the Catholic Church. One way in which it tried to do this was through art. The Church commissioned artists, such as Rubens and Caravaggio, to make grand paintings that would fill the walls of new churches, cathedrals, and chapels across Europe.

The Popes wanted art that the general public could understand and be inspired by. They no longer wanted art in churches to refer back to classical art. They felt this kind of art was mainly appreciated by scholars. They began to commission paintings and sculptures depicting vivid and dramatic images of saints and miracles, with strong contrasts of light and shade. This style became known as the **Baroque**.

Master of drama

Caravaggio was a master of Baroque painting. He was very unusual in his approach. Caravaggio often painted works depicting biblical scenes, such as St. Peter carrying a cross or the Virgin Mary dying. However, he made the images incredibly real by making the figures resemble people he knew from Rome, such as street children and beggars, and putting them in recognizable contemporary street settings.

Michelangelo Merisi da Caravaggio, *Supper at Emmaus* (1601). Caravaggio shows a scene in which followers of Jesus recognize him in their midst. One startled character is gripping his chair and has a shocked face. It is almost as if someone has taken a flash photograph of action on a stage.

The poses and expressions of Caravaggio's subjects look very natural, but they are carefully chosen to capture a moment in time. His technique was also very distinctive, because he used lots of chiaroscuro. Sometimes his figures appear to be emerging from the darkness into blinding light. He used intense highlights to guide the eye of the viewer to what was happening in his images.

Women artists in the Renaissance

In Renaissance times, there were very few opportunities for girls to learn to paint, or for women to train as artists. The women who did learn to paint were generally from rich families or were daughters of master painters. Sofonisba Anguissola, from Cremona in Italy, was the first noted Renaissance female artist. She became a court painter for the Spanish royal family.

Artemisia Gentileschi, from Rome, is the most famous female artist from the seventeenth century. She learned from her father how to paint in the Baroque style of Caravaggio. When she moved to Florence, she started to get commissions and became the first woman ever accepted in the prestigious Academy of Drawing in Florence in 1616. Her dramatic biblical scenes, such as *Judith Slaying Holofernes*, are still well known today.

Sofonisba Anguissola, *Portrait of a Child* (undated). Born in 1532, Sofonisba was the first female artist to gain an international reputation, and she was particularly famous for her portraits.

The Influence of Renaissance Art

Millions of people each year crowd around the *Mona Lisa* in the Louvre Museum, Paris, France.

The influence of Renaissance art is still strong for many artists around the world. For art lovers today, Renaissance paintings and sculptures are still highly valued and represent one of the highest points of artistic excellence.

Today's techniques

Many oil painters today use techniques that were first developed by Renaissance artists.

Artists of today:
- plan their work with carefully observed sketches
- create compositions using linear and color perspective techniques
- use oil paints or the more modern acrylic paints
- use chiaroscuro and sfumato to blend colors and tones, creating shading that makes objects appear solid and three-dimensional.

In Renaissance times, most artists learned about painting and sculpting techniques through lengthy art training. Nowadays, it is rare for artists to train as apprentices to masters, as in Renaissance times, but most artists today follow a similar path of building up skills under art experts at schools or colleges.

The Renaissance approach

During the Renaissance, artists came to be viewed in a different way. Instead of being regarded just as craftsmen, as they were in medieval times, individual painters and sculptors became famous and wealthy during their own lifetimes. Great masters, such as Michelangelo and Leonardo da Vinci, were hailed as creative geniuses. This change in the way artists were treated had a lasting influence.

During the Renaissance, artists became skillful through the study of classical art. Later generations of artists have also revisited classical themes. For example, the great twentieth-century Spanish artist, Pablo Picasso, made images based on the Greek minotaur myth and the Roman god Pan.

The popularity of Renaissance art

Renaissance art is still very popular with art lovers throughout the world. Millions of tourists visit Florence each year. One of the main reasons for this is that visitors can see a variety of Renaissance art, not only in galleries, but also in churches, cathedrals, and historic houses and palaces. Exhibitions of Renaissance art in galleries and museums all over the world are frequently visited.

Renaissance paintings and sculptures today are very valuable. In 2006, two paintings by the Florentine monk, Fra Angelico, made for the Medici family in Florence, were discovered hanging in the spare bedroom in a house in Oxford, U.K. They are now worth millions of dollars!

Renaissance artists of today

Some artists today choose to paint works in the Renaissance style. For example, the U.S. artist, Kurt Wenner, moved to Rome in 1982 to study Renaissance art and classical sculpture. His images feature historical themes, linear and color perspective, and extreme foreshortening.

Unlike Renaissance artists, Wenner creates images not only with paint on canvas, but also with chalk on sidewalks. His street art is much photographed and very popular.

Getting into Art

Would you like to be the next Michelangelo? Want to study and draw from nature like Leonardo? Are you influenced by classical art? Then maybe you want to learn how to create art like the Renaissance masters and make art your career.

Learning from Renaissance sculpture

Renaissance artists learned to depict the human form in a realistic way by copying the techniques of classical sculptors. Many museums have examples of Renaissance sculpture that you can copy. Roughly measure the body proportions so the figure looks right. Try to show the form of the figure by drawing the bulge of muscles, the depth of eye sockets, and the subtle curves of body parts using chiaroscuro and sfumato.

Drawing from nature

Renaissance artists also learned to depict things realistically by drawing directly from nature. You can also take your sketchbook into your backyard, a local park or woods, a zoo, a wildlife park, or a forest preserve. Try to draw nature as you see it. Remember, you have an advantage over Renaissance artists—you can use a camera to capture reality. It is often easier to draw animals, trees, flowers, clouds, and other natural objects from photographs, rather than trying to draw from life. Taking several pictures of the same object from different viewpoints really helps you to understand the form.

Try it yourself

Renaissance paint kit

You will need:

- A sketchbook, and charcoal or pencil—to make careful sketches of the shapes you want to paint

- Oil or acrylic paints—oil dries much more slowly, but the advantage of acrylics is that you can wash out brushes with water

- Brushes—different widths of brush, some soft and others hard

- A palette—to mix your paint colors on

- Canvases—you can stretch them yourself, but it is easier to buy them ready prepared

- An easel—to rest the canvas on as you paint.

Careers in art

Some people with art training become artists, but just as in the Renaissance, it is difficult for artists to find regular commissions and sell their art. So artists often have other careers that use their art skills. Some work in auction houses, using their knowledge of art styles to recognize, value, and sell works of art. Some become art historians, who learn about the world in the past and how social conditions affected what art was produced then. Others may restore old paintings and sculptures, and learn about the science of preserving delicate old pieces of art. A few may use their knowledge of art to work in the movie industry, for example, creating sets and costumes for movies set in Renaissance times.

Some artists use their skills and knowledge to follow a career in art restoration. This woman is carefully painting over missing or damaged sections of a fresco in a chapel in Poland.

Major Renaissance Artists

Hieronymus Bosch (ca. 1450–1516)

The Dutch painter Bosch was famous for his detailed pictures full of weird demons and monsters that showed the wickedness of humans. His paintings make great use of color, and although the subjects are often quite confusing, the pictures are fascinating.

Donatello (Donato di Niccolo) (ca. 1386–1466)

The Italian Renaissance sculptor Donatello worked for 30 years at the cathedral in Florence, where he developed his skills and style. He was an expert in traditional classical style, but developed new ideas about perspective, which he used in his sculptures made in wood, bronze, and stone. His figures were realistic because he studied people in real life to produce them.

Sandro Botticelli (1445–1510)

Botticelli was one of the greatest painters of the Italian Renaissance. He lived most of his life in Florence, where he was one of the city's busiest artists. He painted mainly for the wealthy Medici family and made huge paintings with mythological themes. Unfortunately, by the end of his life, Botticelli had fallen out of favor.

Caravaggio (Michelangelo Merisi da Caravaggio) (1571–1610)

Caravaggio is one of the best-known Baroque artists. He went to Rome at the age of 20 to become a painter, and after a few years as a struggling artist, he started to get commissions from the Church. He painted religious characters that looked real because he used real people as models. He used light and shade to make some parts of his pictures stand out from the background more than others. By the age of 30, Caravaggio's name was known all over Europe. He was known not only for his skill as a painter, but also for his way of life. He was accused of assault several times when in Rome, and in 1606, he killed a man after a dispute over a game of tennis. He fled the city and spent the remaining years of his life traveling from one place to another.

Albrecht Dürer (1471–1528)

A German painter and engraver, Dürer worked for four years with a book illustrator in Germany before traveling to Italy to study the work of Renaissance artists. He worked in different mediums, but is most famous for his engravings and his woodblock prints.

Jan van Eyck (ca. 1395–1441)

The Flemish painter Van Eyck was one of the leading Renaissance artists in northern Europe. He developed and perfected the technique of painting using oils instead of egg tempera. His paintings are small, very detailed, and richly colored.

Leonardo da Vinci (1452–1519)

When he was young, Leonardo trained under an artist who taught him sculpture, painting, and design. By the age of 20, Leonardo was considered a master painter. He was also a scientist and inventor who was fascinated by the world around him; for example, he studied plants and insects for hours with a magnifying glass. As a painter, Leonardo developed the technique known as sfumato in his paintings and solved the problem of how to make faces look three-dimensional on a flat canvas.

Michelangelo Buonarroti (1475–1564)

Michelangelo Buonarroti was an outstanding painter, sculptor, and architect from near Florence. He started working for the Medici family from the age of 14. He considered himself a sculptor, having created such works in Florence as *David* (1504), but one of his best-known works is the painting on the ceiling of the Sistine Chapel in Rome.

Raphael (Raffaello Santi) (1483–1520)

Raphael started training as an artist with his father when he was only seven years old. By the age of 17, he was a master painter. He worked on the Vatican and the Sistine Chapel, as well as making wall paintings, portraits, engravings, and tapestry designs. He was particularly concerned with making people look real and human, with natural expressions and gestures.

Titian (Tiziano Vecelli) (1485–1576)

As a young man, Titian trained under Bellini, a very famous Venetian painter. When Bellini died, Titian took his job as the city's official painter. He made paintings for the great churches and families of Venice. He used bold-colored oil paints and arranged his pictures in new ways, such as putting the subjects in the corner rather than the center of the frame.

Renaissance Art Timeline

1304   Giotto paints frescoes in Padua, some of the first in Italy since classical times

1309   The Popes make their base in Avignon, France

1377   Pope Gregory XI returns to Rome from France

1384   Bruges in present-day Belgium starts to become a major trading center and port when rich French dukes settle there

1386   Donatello is born

1410   Pope John XXIII is elected in Rome with the financial help of the Medici family

1412   The Medici family become the official Papal bankers

1420   Brunelleschi designs a dome for Florence Cathedral by studying the ruins of ancient buildings in Rome

1422   Van Eyck becomes an official court painter in Bruges

1435   Alberti completes *On Painting*, a book with clear instructions on how to use linear perspective

1437   Cosimo de Medici opens the world's first public library at San Marco

1445   Botticelli is born

1448   Fra Angelico creates frescoes for the Vatican palace

1450   Johannes Gutenburg publishes the first printed book—the Bible

1452   Leonardo da Vinci is born

1473   The Medici's bank begins to lose money

1475   Michelangelo is born

1478   Botticelli paints the *Primavera*

1481   Leonardo da Vinci leaves Florence to work for the Duke of Milan, of the Sforza family

1485   Botticelli paints *The Birth of Venus*

1494   Michelangelo flees Florence after Savonarola seizes control

1495   Bosch creates triptychs in 's-Hertogenbosch, in the Netherlands; a printing press is set up in Venice, which becomes the book publishing center of Europe; Albrecht Dürer visits Italy and experiences classical art and Italian painting

1497   Savonarola initiates the Bonfire of the Vanities in Florence

1501 Michelangelo returns to Florence to carve his famous sculpture *David*, intended to be mounted high on Florence Cathedral

1503 Michelangelo's *David* is unveiled outside the Palazzo Vecchio, Florence; Leonardo begins his painting the *Mona Lisa*

1506 Leonardo completes the *Mona Lisa*

1508 Michelangelo begins his painting of the Sistine Chapel ceiling

1510 Botticelli dies; Raphael paints *The School of Athens*, showing an imaginary meeting of famous Greek philosophers

1516 Titian paints his first masterpiece, *Assumption of the Virgin*

1519 Leonardo da Vinci dies in France

1527 Rome is invaded by the forces of King Charles V of France; many artists flee; Michelangelo's *David* is broken in the fighting

1529 The "Protestation" of German followers of Luther is published, coining the term *Protestant*

1534 Luther publishes the Bible in German

1541 Michelangelo's fresco *Last Judgement* is unveiled in the Sistine Chapel

1543 Michelangelo's *David* is restored

1550 Vasari publishes the *Lives of the Artists,* which is a book of accounts of many great Renaissance artists

1551–69 Pieter Bruegel paints peasant landscapes

1564 Michelangelo dies

1591 William Shakespeare's first plays are performed in London

1592 Caravaggio paints the first Baroque paintings

Glossary

altarpiece work of art placed above and behind an altar table in a church

anatomy study of the different parts of the body

Baroque style of art and design that developed in Europe around 1600 and continued to about 1750. Baroque art is characterized by the dramatic use of color and light.

Catholic Church Christian Church that is based in the Vatican, with a Pope as its head

chiaroscuro Italian for "light" (*chiaro*) and "dark" (*oscuro*). It describes the balance of light and shade in a drawing.

classical relating to the ancient Greek and Roman world, especially its art, architecture, literature, and ideas

commission official order for an original piece of work to be created by an artist

composition way in which a painting or other work of art is composed or arranged

contrast range between the darkest and lightest areas in an image

converge come together in the distance. In a drawing that uses perspective, parallel lines appear to converge at a point known as the vanishing point.

court sovereign (such as a king or queen) and their advisers, who form the governing power of a state

doge ruler of Venice in medieval and Renaissance times

egg tempera paint made with pigments mixed with egg and water

engraving print made from a block or plate that has been engraved (when lines are cut into a metal plate and then filled with ink to transfer the image onto paper)

flat two-dimensional, with no depth

Flemish describes the people and lands of Flanders, which in Renaissance times covered parts of present-day Belgium and France

foreshortening form of perspective where the nearest parts of an image are enlarged so that the rest of it looks as if it extends backward into space

fresco type of wall painting. Frescoes were made while the plaster was still fresh (*fresco*) or wet, so that they dried into a long-lasting surface.

geometric relating to simple shapes, such as circles, squares, or triangles

gold leaf very thin sheets of gold foil used as decoration

horizon line line showing the boundary between the land and the sky, usually at the eye level of the viewer

idealized made to look more perfect than in reality

illusion makes something that is not real look real

linear perspective technique of using the illusion that parallel lines meet at a point on the horizon. It is used by artists to give a sense of depth and volume in a flat painting or drawing.

Mannerism artistic style that developed around 1520 and continued to about 1600, in which artists used distorted or elongated figures, and intense lighting and color

medieval another word for Middle Ages, the period in European history roughly between CE 450 and 1450

medium material or art form that an artist can use, such as different types of paint

mosaic design consisting of small pieces of stone, glass, or metal

naturalistic accurately represented as it appears in nature

oil paint paint made from ground pigments mixed with linseed oil

orthogonal line literally, a line that is at right angles to another line. In drawings that use linear perspective, an orthogonal line is the line that extends from the corner of an object to the vanishing point.

patron wealthy person who gives financial support and encouragement to an artist by commissioning them to create works of art

perspective technique used by artists to give depth to a flat or two-dimensional picture, for example, by painting figures smaller to suggest they are farther away

pigment substance that gives paint its color

Pope head of the Roman Catholic Church

Protestant Christian who is not a member of the Roman Catholic or Orthodox churches

relief sculpture that is attached to, but stands out from, a background made from the same material, such as stone

sfumato technique in painting that blends and blurs colors together so there are no definitive outlines in a picture. The technique was developed by Leonardo da Vinci.

stained-glass window window made up of different pieces of colored glass that form pictures and cast beautiful colored light inside a building

stylized shown in a deliberately artistic way, using a definite style

symbol object, character, figure, or color that stands for, or represents, something else

three-dimensional having depth as well as height and width

tone lightness or darkness of a color

triptych image made up of three sections or wooden panels

Tudor name of the royal family that ruled England from 1485 to 1603

two-dimensional having height and width, but no depth

vanishing point in perspective images, the point on the horizon line at which lines that are parallel seem to meet or converge

woodcut picture made by cutting an image in relief on a wood block and then transferring it to paper

Find Out More

Useful websites

General sites on Renaissance art, with examples of Renaissance works

www.artcyclopedia.com
A large site describing different art movements including Renaissance art. Click on the links to find out information on different Renaissance artists, with many examples of Renaissance works from museums and public galleries.

www.metmuseum.org/toah/intro/atr/08sm.htm
A timeline of art history, with information on the important events in art history throughout the world. If you have ever wondered what kind of art was being produced in other countries outside Italy and Europe during the Renaissance period, click on the region you are interested in.

www.nga.gov/collection/gallery/euro15.shtm
A site from the National Gallery of Art in Washington, D.C., describing the art of Northern Europe in the fifteenth and sixteenth centuries, with links to online tours that give examples of works by Northern Renaissance artists.

www.nga.gov/collection/gallery/ita15.shtm
A site from the National Gallery of Art in Washington, D.C., describing Italian painting in the fifteenth century, with links to online tours on Renaissance art in Florence and Siena.

www.nga.gov/collection/gallery/ita16.shtm
A site from the National Gallery of Art in Washington, D.C., describing Italian painting in the sixteenth century, with links to online tours on Venetian art, Raphael, Titian, and Mannerism.

www.renaissanceconnection.org/artexplorer_timeline.html
A pictorial timeline of the Renaissance. Click on the pictures for further information about the events.

www.wga.hu/frames-e.html?/tours/index.html
A site that includes good photos of a vast range of Renaissance paintings from Italy and other parts of Europe; you can take a wide variety of tours, for example, of Giotto's frescoes, the Sistine Chapel, Renaissance sculpture, and Italian Renaissance painters.

Sites featuring individual artists

www.artchive.com/artchive/V/van_eyck.html
A site describing the life and work of Jan van Eyck, with links to examples of his works.

www.bad-penny.gr/bosch/paintings.php?lang=en
A site describing the life and works of Hieronymus Bosch.

www.christusrex.org/www1/sistine/0-Tour.html
A site on the Sistine Chapel, with links to images of the various parts of Michelangelo's ceiling.

www.ibiblio.org/wm/paint/auth/titian
A web museum site describing the life and works of Titian.

www.mos.org/leonardo
A site from the Museum of Science in Boston, Massachusetts, on the life and works of Leonardo da Vinci.

More books to read

Cole, Alison. *Perspective* (Eyewitness Art). New York: Dorling Kindersley, 1992.

Cole, Alison. *The Renaissance* (Eyewitness). New York: Dorling Kindersley, 2000.

Grey, Christopher. *Leonardo's Shadow: Or, My Astonishing Life as Leonardo Da Vinci's Servant.* New York: Simon Pulse, 2008.

Hancock, Lee. *Lorenzo de Medici: Florence's Great Leader and Patron of the Arts* (Rulers, Scholars, and Artists of Renaissance Europe). New York: Rosen, 2004.

Langley, Andrew. *Da Vinci and his Times* (Eyewitness Guides). New York: Dorling Kindersley, 2006.

Marrafino-Rees, Elizabeth. *The Wedding: An Encounter with Jan van Eyck* (Art Encounters). New York: Watson-Guptill, 2005.

Phillips, John. *Leonardo Da Vinci: The Genius Who Defined the Renaissance* (World History Biographies). Des Moines, IA: National Geographic, 2008.

Taking it further

Why not extend your studies, either by searching the Internet, or by looking in books? You could find out about some other Renaissance artists or present-day artists, such as Kurt Wenner, whose art shows Renaissance influences.

Other suggestions for what you might research on the Internet include:

Abbas ibn Firnas, who invented a flying machine in the Islamic Empire about 2,000 years before Leonardo

Frescoes made between Roman times and the Renaissance, such as in cave churches of Göreme, Turkey.

Places to visit

There are Renaissance works of art in museums and art galleries throughout the world. However, here are some that have large and important collections:

United States: Metropolitan Museum of Art, New York; National Gallery of Art, Washington, D.C.

Italy: the Uffizi Gallery and Pitti Palace, Florence; the Vatican Museum, Rome; the Sistine Chapel, Rome; Accademia, Venice; the Brera, Milan

United Kingdom: Victoria and Albert Museum, London; National Gallery, London

France: Musée du Louvre, Paris

Spain: Prado Museum, Madrid

Index